LIGHT AND SOUND

LIGHT

by Julia Garstecki

a Capstone company — publishers for children

Raintree is an imprint of Capstone Global Library Limited, a company incorporated in England and Wales having its registered office at 264 Banbury Road, Oxford, OX2 7DY – Registered company number: 6695582

www.raintree.co.uk
myorders@raintree.co.uk

Copyright © Capstone Global Library Limited 2022

The moral rights of the proprietor have been asserted. All rights reserved. No part of this publication may be reproduced in any form or by any means (including photocopying or storing it in any medium by electronic means and whether or not transiently or incidentally to some other use of this publication) without the written permission of the copyright owner, except in accordance with the provisions of the Copyright, Designs and Patents Act 1988 or under the terms of a licence issued by the Copyright Licensing Agency, 5th Floor, Shackleton House, 4 Battle Bridge Lane, London, SE1 2HX (www.cla.co.uk). Applications for the copyright owner's written permission should be addressed to the publisher.

ISBN 978 1 3982 0416 4 (hardback)
ISBN 978 1 3982 0417 1 (paperback)

Image Credits
Capstone Studio: Karon Dubke, 15, 20; Shutterstock: Africa Studio, Cover (wood), atsurkan, 17, Designua, 9, George Rudy, 19, Jochen Kost, 7, kosam, 8, Kuki Ladron de Guevara, 11, Mykola Mazuryk, 12, nadiya_sergey, 6, Nasky, 13, PR Image Factory, 16, Roman Yastrebinsky, Cover (lamp), WeAre, 5

Design Elements
Capstone; Shutterstock: Miloje, Nasky

Editorial Credits
Editor: Michelle Parkin; Designer: Ted Williams; Media Researcher: Jo Miller; Production Specialist: Laura Manthe

All internet sites appearing in back matter were available and accurate when this book was sent to press.

British Library Cataloguing in Publication Data
A full catalogue record for this book is available from the British Library.

Printed and bound in India

CONTENTS

WHAT IS LIGHT? 4

LIGHT FROM THE SUN 6

A COLOURFUL WORLD 8

BENDING LIGHT 10

RAINBOW SCIENCE 12

SHADOWS 14

LIGHT AROUND US 16

LIGHT HELPS US 18

CHANGING LIGHT 20

GLOSSARY 22

FIND OUT MORE 23

INDEX 24

Words in **bold** are in the glossary.

WHAT IS LIGHT?

Have you ever woken up in the middle of the night? It is dark. You can't see well in the dark.

Turn on the lamp! Light from the lamp lights up your room. Light helps us to see. But how?

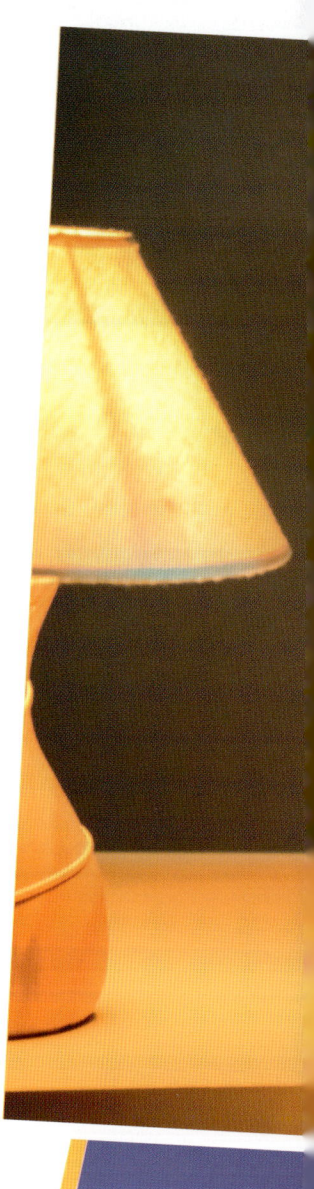

LIGHT FROM THE SUN

Most of the light we see comes from the Sun. It travels here in **waves**. The Sun is about 150 million kilometres away.

Light travels quickly. Light can reach the Earth in 8 minutes and 20 seconds. Nothing is faster than the speed of light.

A COLOURFUL WORLD

A tree's leaves are green. Its trunk is brown. We see these colours because of light. Light hits the tree. Some light is soaked up, or **absorbed**.

Some light bounces off the tree. This light is **reflected** back to us. Reflected light is the colours we see.

BENDING LIGHT

Light travels in a straight line. But some objects can bend the light. Put a pencil in a glass of water. The pencil looks like it is bending. But why?

This is called **refraction**. Light bends when it travels through the water. The pencil isn't bent. It just looks that way!

RAINBOW SCIENCE

Rainbows refract and reflect light. Look up at the sky after it rains. You may see a rainbow.

Light passes through water droplets in the air. These droplets bend the light. This lets us see the rainbow's colours.

SHADOWS

Look behind you on a sunny day. Is something following you on the ground? If you jump, it jumps. If you run, it runs. It's your **shadow**!

Light can't pass through your body. The light that you block makes your shadow. Anything that blocks light has a shadow.

LIGHT AROUND US

We use light every day. Light comes to us from the Sun. We use it to see. Without light it is difficult to play! At night, we can use electric lights to help us see.

Some people need to wear eyeglasses. **Lenses** in the glasses bend the light. They help people to see better.

LIGHT HELPS US

Light waves are all around us. They help us see colours. Some objects absorb light. Others reflect light back to us.

Light helps us to see in the dark. You can use a night light in your room. How does light help you?

CHANGING LIGHT

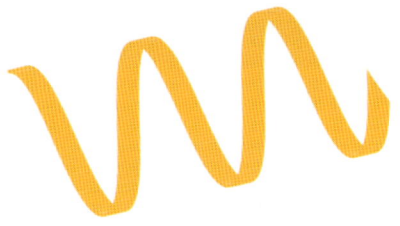

Find out how different objects can change light.

What you need:
- a dark room
- a torch
- an empty glass
- a glass of water
- wax paper
- a piece of cardboard
- a hand mirror

What you do:
1. Find a small room, such as a bathroom.
2. Close the door. Make sure no light can come in from a window.
3. Place the empty glass, glass of water, wax paper, cardboard and hand mirror on a table.
4. Turn off the light.
5. Shine your torch on each item.

Watch how the beam of light changes when it shines on each object. Does the light look the same? Why or why not?

GLOSSARY

absorb to soak up

lens a piece of curved glass or plastic used in eyeglasses

rainbow arc of colours in the sky formed by sunlight shining through drops of water in the air

reflect to return light from an object

refraction the bending of light

shadow the dark shape when something blocks light

wave the energy moving through air or water

FIND OUT MORE

BOOKS

Experiments with Light (Read and Experiment), Isabel Thomas (Raintree, 2015)

Investigating Light (Be a Scientist), Jacqui Bailey (Raintree, 2019)

What is Light? (Science Basics), Mark Weakland (Wayland, 2019).

WEBSITES

Light Facts
www.dkfindout.com/uk/science/light/

What is Light? BBC Bitesize
www.bbc.co.uk/bitesize/topics/zk2pb9q/articles/zmbvgwx

INDEX

absorbing 8, 14, 18

colours 8, 9, 13, 18

eyeglasses 17, 18

light 4, 6, 14, 17

rainbows 12, 13

reflecting 9, 12, 18

refracting 10, 12

shadows 14

speed of light 7

sun 6, 16

uses for light 16, 18